Telepathy for Advanced Learners

Connections, Possibilities and an Old Way

Contact: www.HarryEilenstein.de
Harry.Eilenstein@web.de
Harry Eilenstein at youtube

Production and publishing house: BoD – Books on Demand, Norderstedt

ISBN: 9783753476988

Table of Contents

1. Resolution and Help

1. a) Advanced telepathy

In "Telepathy for Beginners" telepathy itself has been described – how to prove its existence and how it works.

"Telepathy for Advanced" is about how to gain a higher degree of reliability in telepathic perceptions and how to use them consciously in one's own life.

While in "Telepathy for Beginners" only general experiments were presented, with which one can prove telepathy and understand its functioning, in this volume individual experiments and exercises are found, which make it possible to develop one's own telepathic abilities.

1. b) The request for help

Every change begins with the decision to make that change. A solid decision usually has a high degree of clarity: one knows why one decides to do something. This does not mean that one knows many details about the motivation and the planned course of action, but it does mean that the resolution has roots in one's own truth, that it is an expression of who one is at one's core.

The motivation for this resolution need not be a lofty goal such as the redemption of the world from all evil – a lively curiosity about one's own possibilities is quite sufficient.

It is also beneficial if one has an idea of what one wants to do for the achievement of the goal to which the resolution refers – in this case, what one wants to do for the further development of one's own telepathic abilities. Even these ideas do not have to be worked out in detail, but a certain clarity is helpful.

The considerations in "Telepathy for Beginners" have shown that a single telepathic perception is one thread in a large, interconnected "telepathic web" that links all things together.

It is therefore seems natuaral to use this "telepathic fabric" for the further development of one's own telepathic abilities. The procedure for this is quite simple: one telepathically sends out an invitation to all conducive circumstances.

Such an invitation is most effective when it is made within the framework of a simple ritual. Of course, this does not mean that one has to build a temple or erect a stone circle and wear long robes. A ritual can be very simple and is simply an effective way to send a telepathic message.

Such a ritual contains several elements:

Is there a time that particularly suits one's intention? If so, the ritual should be performed at that time.

For particularly large projects Yule (midwinter on 21 December) has proven itself with me to be very effectiv – in this night already the Teutons started all more important projects. At Yule smbolically the sun is reborn, which means that the wish expressed in this night symbolically-magically like the sun in the following half year will grow and prosper (the days become longer = the sun becomes stronger). By expressing the wishes at Yule the wishes receive the strength and support of the sun. From this Germanic custom today only the good resolutions on New Year's Eve are left …

Another good date is full moon, because on this day there is a greater tension than usual – which you can use as an impetus for your own intention.

However, the success of the resolution does not depend on choosing a "right time". The right time can also simply be "Now!".

Is there a place that fits particularly well to your own project? For example, I have a round flokati rug on which I meditate and which I place first on the sweat lodge frame for all the sweat lodges I lead, and which I also use for family constellations and the like. This is my "proper place" in most cases.

The right place can also be a clearing in the forest, a small chapel or simply one's own living room.

Which words express your intention best? They don't have to be perfect, they don't have to be pre-determined, but a little reflection on one's motivation will promote accuracy and thus effectiveness of the words in one's resolution ritual.

Are there gestures that can describe the intention? This can be a raising of the arms (contact with the gods), a gesture of receiving (generally very helpful …), a determined stamping of the feet (will), a pouring of water (letting go), eating a fruit (being nourished) and many other things – the gestures possibly used depend on what one wants to achieve.

Is there a certain clothing that fits to it? This is not an important point, but if there is something suitable, you can wear it at this time.

Is the motivation clear? Sometimes one desires something as a substitute for something else or as a tool to achieve something else.

One sometimes eats a piece of cake because one is lonely – one is lonely because one has separated – one has separated because one has been angry – one has been angry because another person has hurt one – the other person has been able to hurt one because one has not yet healed an old wound … Wishing for a piece of cake is not the most effective resolution in this case …

You might also wish for a car, because it would be faster to get to your girlfriend who lives three towns away. In such a case, it might be helpful to ask yourself why your girlfriend lives so far away and how it would feel if she lived only three houses away.

A clear motivation is the most important thing in a ritual, because the effect of the ritually expressed wish will reflect the motivation – including its clarity or ambiguity.

Only the fulfillment of a wish that is close to one's heart, that is, close to one's truth, makes one really happy. What does the piece of cake help, if one is actually already full? And what good is a car when your girlfriend moves to America three days later? It is important to look for the root of the desires.

This root does not have to be deep and earth-shattering, but simply honest. If you would like to have an ice cream right now, but you don't have any money with you, you can go ahead and wish for an ice cream – see what happens …

Finally, there is another important aspect of ritual wishing: a witness. If you only think something, it remains inside you; if you say it aloud, it is already a little more outside; if you say it in front of a witness, you cannot take it back and it is anchored in the world.

If it suits the resolution, one can perform such a resolution ritual – simply because such a ritual is effective. However, this does not at all mean that only such ritually expressed wishes are effective: If a wish has ripened and one inwardly wishes something all at once on a ride in the subway without any restrictions and without any "ifs and buts", this wish will have a great effect.

The ritual form of wishing is ultimately only a concentration aid … but one that can be quite useful.

If one has come to the conclusion that one wants to learn telepathy, one can consider making such a ritual resolution.

The effect of such a ritual decision cannot be predicted – you may meet someone who also wants to explore telepathy; you may find a book that helps you; you may often find yourself in situations where you need telepathy; you may simply experience telepathy all the time …

You can also look at what you want to do yourself to develop your own telepathic abilities: Doing dream journeys, doing chakra meditations, searching for lost things in a telepathic way … there are many possibilities …

2. The Telepathy Model

2. a) The model from "Telepathy for Beginners

In the first volume telepathy has been described as a single thread in a big whole.

The "place" from which telepathy emanates is the astral body, the substance of which can be called "life force" – simply to have a practical term with which to describe telepathic processes and the like.

This "place" is usually unconscious, so a monitor (pendulum, tarot cards, etc.) can be helpful. Learning telepathy consists essentially of becoming aware of telepathic perceptions (which are already there all the time).

Telepathy is closely related to telekinesis, i.e. "moving by thought", and also to homeopathy and magic.

One can call the level on which the astral body is located and on which telepathy and also telekinesis take place, "astral level" or also "life force level". "Collective subconsciousness" is also a suitable term.

One's own part in this plane is the astral body, which is the part of one's being that "sees telepathically" and that "acts telekinetically".

2. b) One's own model

It is helpful to look at other people's experiments, findings and formulations, but it is equally helpful to then look for one's own description that corresponds to one's own language and world view and expresses one's own experiences and findings.

Maybe a technical "life force internet" would correspond much better to one's own style or a poetic "psyche of mother earth". Maybe one is Pisces by zodiac sign and prefers to speak of universal connections – or one is Scorpio and therefore finds "magical will enforcement" more appropriate.

More important than the choice of words, however, is the clarity about what one has experienced oneself and what one can therefore be sure of.

Ultimately, thinking has the task of figuring out how the world works and then using that knowledge to achieve one's goals – in this way, clarity emerges.

So a well-grounded realism is needed – which also includes telepathy, if one has recognized that it exists.

3. The "Language" of Telepathy

3. a) The "atoms" and "molecules" of telepathy

Telepathy takes place on the level of the subconscious but can also be perceived consciously with a little practice. On the level of the subconscious there are other structures than in the area of the waking consciousness, in which the causal logic ("if – then") prevails. The subconscious is mainly structured by association.

An association is, for example, the connection between "hunger" and "food". Such associations usually do not stand alone – for example, "kitchen" and "stove" and many others also belong to the mentioned example.

The elements that are associatively connected are usually images. They can be rather neutral or charged with feelings. The term belonging to the picture is usually only loosely connected to the picture.

The single picture is, so to speak, the "atom" on the level of the life force. An association complex like the four example terms just mentioned would then be a "molecule" on the life force level.

There are also "cells" which consist of a large number of "molecules". In the association cell "mother" there are besides the above mentioned "nutrition" also the association molecules "security", "protection", "breast", "milk", "family", "siblings", "childhood" and some more.

The images that form the content of the subconscious are organized in several stages by association: small units ("hunger and food"), medium units ("nourishment"), and large units ("mother"). Of course, these do not always have to be three levels of organization, but they can just as well be two or five levels – the example is only meant to illustrate the general structure of the inner imagery.

These inner pictures and their association logic can be experienced e.g. in dreams. These image-association complexes give rise to symbols, i.e. groups of related images with a definite quality, but without a sharp boundary towards the outside. Such symbols are also constantly used in religion and magic.

The knowledge of these inner images and the associative logic by which they are connected is also beneficial in telepathy – although telepathy of course works without this knowledge. However, when using e.g. dream journeys to learn telepathy, it is extremely helpful to be able to understand the images one perceives. However, it also depends on the subject of the dream journeys whether one sees concrete pictures or symbolic pictures.

The associations are in a way the "language of the moon", because astrologically the moon is one's own subconsciousness.

Also with telepathic-telekinetic healings etc. one can use this picture-language.

For example, one can imagine fire in the root chakra during an attack of weakness, since fire is the general symbol for the life force. One experiences its movements as heat (kundalini) – in Africa, the life force is therefore called "life fire" ("Kalifi") in some cultures.

In all kinds of confusion or inner contradictions, one can imagine a sun in the heart chakra, because the sun is the general symbol of the radiant center and of the soul.

With the feeling of disorientation or meaninglessness, one can imagine dazzling white light in the crown chakra, because this form of light is the general symbol for God or for the unity behind the multiplicity of the world.

These three symbols are found in almost all cultures because they are based on fundamental experiences in everyday life. Other such symbols include the soul bird (experience of astral travel), the mother goddess in cow form (milk of the cow), and the large predator (power).

A complete presentation of this imagery and the "language of the moon" resulting from it, however, would fill a book of its own – see, if you are interested, my book "The Language of the Moon – for Beginners".

3. b) One's own "Language of the Moon"

For the learning of telepathy and especially for the correct interpretation of the images that may appear, it is helpful to get to know one's own inner imagery. For this it is again beneficial to look at one's own dreams, one's own dream journeys, the omens occurring in one's own life (meaningful coincidences etc.) and the oracles one has used (Tarot, I Ching) etc. from time to time.

To be able to do this it is helpful to write down one's own dreams, dream journeys, oracle results etc. and to look at them from time to time. In doing so, one looks for repetitions, for similarities, for images that often occur together and therefore seem to form a common theme.

It is also important to be able to distinguish what are general symbolisms and what are individual symbolisms.

The motif of the mother goddess, who in the afterlife gives re-birth to the soul-birds, and who can therefore also have the form of a bird herself, is common throughout the world. Likewise, the motif of the life-giving potion, which also gives rebirth, is also found in very many cultures – this is a reinterpretation of mother's milk. Also the transformation into a large predator is found in many myths – this is the successful identification with the large predator, by which one can obtain the power of this animal (a very old kind of hunting magic).

On the other hand, the association between a rose and death would be distinctly individual – perhaps one has lost a dear person who liked roses and one has therefore planted a rose bush on his grave.

The at least rough knowledge of one's own images and also of the mythological motifs spread all over the world are not directly necessary for learning telepathy, but the knowledge of these images helps to avoid misunderstandings and misinterpretations which could lead to unhelpful actions.

If one extends telepathy to magic, e.g., using symbols in rituals with which one wants to achieve a specific effect, it is important to know the symbols used, since the effect of magic is usually more strongly influenced by the symbols used than by the conscious intention.

Symbols are the "words" of the collective subconsciousness …

4. The "Telepathy Level"

4. a) Structure and dynamics

In the earlier magical-mythological worldviews, the gods were the most important beings on the "telepathic plane" – one could also say that they have been the most important images on this plane. They are, in a way, the cornerstones of the structures on this plane.

The myths that were told about these gods were a reflection of the dynamics in this "inner structure".

This level still exists today, it is only no longer the "official world picture", but is hidden as the "collective subconscious" under the level of logic and natural sciences.

A really existing level of the world, which is no longer observed or of which it is even said that it does not exist at all, could cause problems, because it works, but is not seen and not understood. This does not mean that one should now become religious as quickly as possible, but merely that it makes sense to ask oneself once what one knows about this plane.

As almost always, experiments are the best tool to learn more about an unknown area. For the subject under consideration here, dream journeys to various deities are the most obvious. In doing so, one can ask the deities about anything or ask them for help for anything.

For example, I have been thinking for more than ten years about what actually caused the failure of the cooperative that ran the organic food store in which I was a co-owner for 20 years: How did one individual manage to seize all the power, drive everyone else away, and become a sole proprietor who owns the health food store. When I made a dream journey to the German judge-god Forseti for my series of books on the Germanic gods, I asked him about it – I suspected that as a judge-god he would be familiar with legal matters and with disputes.

He then explained to me that we had been a group of people with victim mentality, protecting each other from the world. Then, when a "wolf in sheep's clothing" came into our "flock of sheep" and quietly gained a position of power, we "sheep" could not defend ourselves against the wolf when we realized what was under the sheep's clothing. Forseti told me that cooperatives only work when they are run by a group of people who are neither victim-sheep nor perpetrator-wolves, but who rest in themselves and use their power with serenity and purpose.

These conversations with the gods can therefore also be extremely helpful in every-day life. The same is true, of course, when one asks a god or goddess not for advice but for help.

Such experiences form the basis for an "expanded world view" in which gods also appear as very real sources of advice and help. First of all, it doesn't matter what gods actually are – the essential point is that they can make one's life easier.

These conversations with the gods can also be technically called "telepathic information gathering" – which is, however, a somewhat unwieldy term that does not at all reflect the feeling during such conversations with gods and goddesses.

Of course, one should not simply believe everything one hears during these conversations – after all, one does not know in the first place where the information one has heard comes from. Therefore one should always consider whether one follows e.g. an advice or not. With increasing experience, the skeptical attitude of experimentation will give way to trust – but one should never give up one's own judgment, otherwise one could easily get caught up in unrealistic ideas, in dependencies, in compulsive actions, and the like.

The center of one's own actions, i.e. one's soul, should always remain one's own center, even if one has experienced that one is connected to the world in a variety of ways – including telepathy to other people, animals, plants, gods, homeopathic beads, planets, and much more.

4. b) One's own mythology

When one has dealt with one's own inner images and has become somewhat more familiar with them, and when one has made contact with some deities, one can begin to explore the relationships between one's own inner images and also their connections to the deities. The core of one's mythology is one's soul, one's power animal, one's power plant and one's power stone.

In order to recognize this mythology of one's own life, it also helps to look at what things one experiences again and again, what fears and addictions one has, what one's life plan looks like and what one's horoscope says about it.

This own mythology is not a static structure that cannot be changed. However, it cannot be changed arbitrarily either – after all, you keep the same horoscope all your life. However, you can change the level at which you live your own horoscope. This also changes one's own life story and mythology.

For example, if you have a square between Pluto and Saturn in your chart, you will generally have a separation (square) between the essential (Pluto) and the permanent (Saturn) in your own life.

However, one can live this constellation in many different ways:

1. as a suburban gangster who does what he wants (Pluto) and doesn't care (square) about the law (Saturn);

2. after that, the person may be in jail, where the law (Saturn) doesn't care (square) what the gangster wants (Pluto);

3. after release from jail, the subject might become a social critic (Pluto criticizes Saturn);

4. maybe he withdraws (square) from the world (Saturn) and meditates (Pluto);

5. possibly he then becomes a healer or spiritual teacher (Pluto), who stands outside (square) of any traditional orders (Pluto);

6. then people establish a monastery (Saturn) for him, but this becomes too narrow (square) for him (Pluto),

7. so that he becomes a hermit, turns away (square) from the world (Saturn) and becomes enlightened (Pluto) …

The exploration of one's own inner mythology helps to send out telepathically what one really wants – and no longer to send out one's own fears and addictions, whereby what one fears comes to one and what one longs for stays away.

The problem with telepathy is that it always works – you send out into the world the images you carry within you, and thereby call forth an echo to the images you carry within you. Consequently, in order to obtain what one really wants, it is necessary to recognize and heal the inner images.

Therefore, learning telepathy is not learning the ability to send out something telepathically, but on the one hand to heal the inner images so that one lets one's heart and not one's own fears and addictions radiate out into the world, and on the other hand to become aware of this telepathic sending. When one has achieved this, one is able to telepathically call forth that which truly delights one's heart.…

Then one has become a magician.

5.   Contact and Analogy

5. a)   The "telepathic environment"

The question arises, how free one's own will and telepathy actually are. One's own life is fixed in its basic structure by one's own horoscope and also one's own power animal, power plant and power stone remain the same throughout life. Now the soul, the horoscope, the power animal, the power plant and the power stone are however nothing, which stands on the outside, but inside the own identity.

> The soul is what has incarnated and what has chosen the present life.

> The horoscope is the quality that the soul chooses to explore in its current incarnation.

> The power animal is the animal that is most similar in dynamic to the incarnational impulse of one's soul.

> The power plant is the plant that is most similar in posture to the incarnational impulse of one's soul.

> The power stone is the stone which is most similar in structure to the incarnation impulse of one's own soul.

These five beings or things are an expression of one's own identity and therefore unchangeable for this life. They are that, what wants to radiate, what wants to be expressed, what wants to take shape. This radiation, which is as unhindered as possible, is ultimately what constitutes happiness.
This radiating is telepathy, which is connected to one's own heart chakra and radiates from it into the world.
The sun of the soul in one's own heart chakra shapes the images of the moon area of one's own life force, which in turn telepathically draws to itself from the world that which fits these images.

At this point begins the area where one can change and shape one's own life:

> As long as one lives in the attitude of a lack, one will either shout loudly and become an addict, or get more and more silent and become an ascetic. Both deviate from the whole center of trust and safety – and therefore telepathically call the opposite pole into one's own life: the helpful ascetic needs

the needy addict – and vice versa.

As long as one lives in the attitude of danger, one will either shout loudly and become a perpetrator, or get more and more silent and become a victim. Both deviate from the whole center of power and serenity – and therefore telepathically call the opposite pole into one's own life: the power-hungry perpetrator needs the powerless victim – and vice versa.

As long as one lives in the attitude of self-uncertainty, one will either shout loudly and become a star, or get more and more silent and become a fan. Both of them deviate from the whole center of self-love and radiance – and therefore telepathically call the opposite pole into one's own life: the megalomaniac star needs the fan with the inferiority complex – and vice versa.

These six basic "sick" inner images (addict and ascetic, perpetrator and victim, star and fan) shape the images one telepathically sends out into the world.

For example, the more extreme the victim attitude is, the more extreme things one will experience with violence by other people.

And the more one dissolves and heals this victim attitude, the more peaceful and balanced one's own life will become.

There is another consideration about telepathy which is important in this context: The course of the planets is already fixed for the future – and accordingly also the horoscopes of the people who will be born in the future. Also one's own life is shaped by one's own horoscope – and furthermore also by the relation of the planets which are at a certain day up in the sky to the planets in one's own horoscope ("astrological transits").

The script is already written, the course of one's own life is already fixed in its structure – where is freedom?

The answer is the same as in the previous consideration: One cannot change the fact that the next full moon comes with its own tension, and one cannot change the fact that at the age of 28 Saturn stands again where it stood at the time of birth and thus clearly shows to each person what he has made of his life so far – but one can live out these cycles and currents, which can be described by astrology, on different levels.

For example, one can become frantic on any full moon, but one can also consciously make a change in disagreeable circumstances in one's life on every full moon – the experience of the full moon becomes completely different.

One can become depressed during the "Saturn phase" at about 28, but one can also take a close look at what one has been formed into so far by one's own resolutions – and make decisions for one's future life.

Thus, there are structures which are already fixed: one's own soul and the "cycles of the life force" which can be described by astrology. The soul wants to radiate from the inside to the outside and to call telepathically into one's own life what suits it and by which it can express itself in the most fulfilling way. The astrologically describable "cycles of the life force" give the quality in the world in which the soul wants to radiate.

Both effects, i.e. the radiation of the soul and the cycles of the life force, can be understood as telepathy: both are a non-material effects – the radiation of the soul calls into one's own life what just fits to it (and also to the possible images of fear and addiction in the psyche), and by the state of the planets one can recognize which "weather" just prevails in the area of the life force.

The individual conscious or semi-conscious sending or receiving of telepathy is always related to and happens against the background of these two things: the radiating of the soul from within into the cycles of the life force outside.

5. b) One's own "telepathic environment"

The advice here is again the same as in the previous chapters: "Know thyself."

To implement this recommendation, which is written above the gate of the Oracle Temple of Delphi, in one's own life, one can make dream journeys to one's own soul, dance one's own power animal, have one's horoscope interpreted – and above all listen into oneself to feel what is in one, where one is sincere and serene, where fearful and where addicted … and then see how one can promote what feels good, and how one can heal what feels sick.

Also the second inscription above the gate of the Oracle Temple of Delphi is very useful: "Nothing in excess." This helps to heal the inner image of the addict and the ascetic, of the perpetrater and the victim, and of the star and the fan.

Developing one's telepathic abilities is ultimately a self-healing process more than anything else.

6. Conscious and Unconscious Telepathy

6. a) Security

Learning telepathy is very different from learning e.g. physics or economics: In ordinary learning, one must look at the outside world, perform experiments in the outside, memorize things, and then be able to apply the knowledge. In learning telepathy, one must look at one's inner world, perform experiments on the inside, discover one's mythology, and then live this mythology at the highest possible level in the outer world.

When learning a natural science, one's gaze is mainly directed outward to the world – when learning telepathy, one's gaze is mainly directed inward to one's own life force, astral body and soul.

When learning a natural science, one is interested but distant – the formula "$E=mc^2$" is very interesting, but its understanding does not change much one's own state of mind.

When learning telepathy, on the other hand, one is both interested and involved. The realization of which "sea of a deity" one's soul is a "drop" shows to which deity one has the closest connection. The mythology of this deity is also the mythology of one's own life. Therefore the discovery of the deity, which is the "father" or "mother" of one's own soul, may change one's attitude towards life to a very great extent.

The external world considered by natural sciences always behaves in the same way, which makes it quite easy to formulate objective and universally valid descriptions.

With telepathy, on the other hand, one is dealing with an area which can be made conscious, but in which many things happen unconsciously, which is why it is not so easy to make generally valid statements – and where an accurate description of one's own, completely subjective situation is usually also much more interesting.

Since telepathy often runs unconsciously, at least in the time when one is still learning to become more aware of one's own inner self, it often happens that one intuitively says or does something meaningful and does not know where the impulse for these words or this action came from.

In addition, pleasant "meaningful coincidences" occur again and again, which sometimes occur "just like that" even without one's own wishes.

This unconscious telepathy, which enriches one's life, has its root in the radiance of one's own soul – in its desire for self-expression. This unconscious telepathy can therefore lead to the experience of security in the world:

The world reflects back to you what you are radiating;

that, what one radiates, one can change by self-knowledge, which in turn changes the external events;

and the soul radiates within oneself and one only needs to allow its light to radiate unhindered outward into one's life in order to become happy.

One only needs to allow oneself to be oneself ….

This arrangement on the level of the life force leads to the fact that one is safe in the world – it always happens what fits to oneself, one always receives what fits to what one radiates into the world.

Therefore, one "only" needs to dissolve one's own fears and addictions and self-doubts in order to receive what corresponds to one's own truth in one's own heart chakra.

6. b) Trust and responsibility

The consideration in the previous section shows that one is responsible for what one experiences: the inner images telepathically summon from the outside what fits these inner images. One is the architect of one's own happiness …

At the same time, however, this responsibility results in a trust in the world – precisely because things do not happen by chance, but depend on the radiance of one's own heart and on the cycles of the life force – and on the level to which one has raised one's own self-expression, i.e. how much one has already healed from one's own fears and addictions and self-doubts.

Trust and responsibility both arise from a connectedness with the world – and telepathy is a "non-material connectedness" of a human being with another human being or animal, plant or thing. Trust means that one is carried by the world – responsibility means that one carries the world.

Trust and responsibility are thus two qualities or behaviors that arise directly from the experience of telepathy – and which therefore in turn also promote the further development of telepathy.

The way to get there is always the same: look at yourself, be friendly to yourself, look at what is conspicuous in your own life and see where it fits into your own picture and in what way it makes sense.

By this form of serene, radiant attention, you heal yourself, you find your way, and you incidentally attain greater and greater awareness in telepathy.

7. The Freely Available Information

7. a) Models of the "big picture"

The model of the "big whole" is found in many religions and world views: God in the monotheistic religions, the Tao of the Chinese, the Being of the philosophers, the Unity of the mystics, the collective subconsciousness in psychology, and many more.

The more experimental representatives of the most diverse religions, i.e. the shamans, mystics, yogis, Sufis, etc., have striven to experience this "great whole" directly. From this aspiration, various descriptions of the path to this goal have gradually emerged, all of which have in common that they are described as a path with various stages: the ladder of heaven of the Christian mystics, the rose path of the Sufis, the yoga system of the yogis, the Lamrim ("step path") of the Tibetan lamas, the Kabbalistic Tree of Life of the Jewish mystics, the step pyramids in Mesopotamia, China and Central America, etc.

On this path, there is a stage where a form of omniscience arises – more precisely, a transparency of the world, on the basis of which one can obtain all information. At this stage one obviously reaches the "perfect telepathy".

While in astral travel one leaves one's own body and travels with one's own consciousness and one's own perceptive faculty outside to the place one wants to see, on the Step-Way one travels inside to the unity of the world, to God – and on the way one reaches a place where the world becomes transparent and where nothing is hidden anymore.

This place is always in the same place in the different systems: The path always begins with one's own body, leads through one's own psyche to one's own soul, then into the realm of the gods and finally to the one God. The place where all information is accessible to the wanderer on the ladder of heaven is at the upper border of the realm of the souls – where this realm meets the realm of the deities.

This location results from the inner logic of the Step-Way. The five main steps on this way and the four main transitions on this way are:

> In the realm of the body everything is separated. Here one sees with the physical eyes and things are illuminated from the outside.

>> At the transition from the outside to the inside one beginns to see inner images, to imagine inner pictures in magic, to use telepathy and telekinesis.

> In the realm of the psyche, things are associated with each other, i.e. telepathically connected. Here one sees the inner images, which are mostly color-

less shadows and are in a realm of diffuse light that has no discernible source.

At the transition from the realm of the psyche to the realm of the soul, one sees single images without motion, that begin to glow in color from within; the contours of the images become extremely sharp; and all forms are constantly changing.

The realm of souls consists of the centers of people, animals and all other beings. Here things shine from within and are colored.

A rather striking quality is also found at the transition from the realm of the souls to the realm of the gods. The soul rests in itself and is filled with self-love – it can therefore look at everything that is inside and outside of the soul. The soul is able look at everything without fear. The closer one gets to the realm of the gods, the more one sees – inside and outside.

- In a first stage one sees not only the character of one's own soul, but also its motivation for its present life and finally its past incarnations.
- This unobstructed self-awareness of the soul is followed in a second stage by the realization of the soul's motivation that led it to its present incarnation.
- In a third stage may be found the recollection of all incarnations of the soul.

This widening of the vision finally leads to the fact that the radius of its perception becomes unlimited.

This unlimited perception is the prerequisite for taking the next step – only when one can calmly contemplate everything that there is, one will be able to enter the realm of the gods and give up all delimitation and anchor one's identity in one's own quality and no longer in one's own delimitation.

This unlimited perception is first experienced as the "transparency" of the entire world – nothing is hidden anymore, everything has become effortlessly telepathically visible … After that oneself becomes part of a continuum – one has reached the realm of the gods.

In the realm of the gods there are no more boundaries, no delimitations, but only qualities that can overlap – gods are unlimited like light. Here one sees contours in the light.

At the transition from the gods to God one says a comprehensive "yes" to everything. This may be experienced as the tranition from an area of light-storm to a sudden blazing white light, which is the one and the only and all.

In the realm that represents God, there is only unity, the one blazing white light.

In order to reach comprehensive telepathy, i.e. omniscience, one must first become prepared to see and know everything – which is not as easy as it may sound, since this knowledge includes, besides all hidden fears, addictions and self-doubts, e.g. also all the cruel deeds in the world and also the date of one's own death in one's own present incarnation.

The boundlessness of the realm of deities is Buddha's criterion by which he describes an enlightened one who is thus a "wanderer in the world of the gods." In Buddha's teaching, this state is associated with the attainment of the four "limitless qualities" of an enlightened person:

- boundless serenity (equanimity, accepting everything, affirming everything),
-boundless compassion (the realization that everything is interconnected),
- boundless love (the egoism extended to the whole world) and
- boundless joy (the experience of unity underlying multiplicity).

It would be practical, of course, if one could give detailed instructions on how to enter this realm. There are, of course, the yoga teachings mentioned at the beginning, the Tibetan Lamrim, the Rose Path of the Sufis, the Kabbalistic Tree of Life, etc., which all agree with each other in their basic features, but since people are all very different, there are general descriptions, but no universal "recipe" that works always and for everyone – the path to this "perfect telepathy" is individual for everyone.

One of the greatest helps on this path is experiencing this state with another person. But it is also possible to reach this experience without a role model or guru.

However, the description of these ways requires too much space to be inserted in this book – I have presented the way of the Kabbalistic Tree of Life in the three volumes "Blüten des Lebensbaumes".

7. b) A dream journey on the Cabbalistic Tree of Life

It seems to me to be the easiest way to present the just described "transparent" area, in which all information is accessible, in a more or less vivid way, to describe the dream journey, on which I reached this area for the first time.

My friend Jörg and I undertook this dream journey about 15 years ago, because I had come to the conclusion that, in order to be able to get along in my life, I would have to know why my soul actually decided to live this life of all things and to create such a strange Harry.

The dream journey began with me going back in my memory first in five-year steps and then in year steps towards birth, telling Jörg at each step where I am at the moment. Since I could already remembered my birth at that time, the way back to that point was quite easy. Jörg had only isolated, fleeting images of my life in this part and felt rather left out.

At first the perception from the time before my birth was as one would imagine it: dim light, warm, weightless, no breathing, eating or drinking of my own – rather resting and waiting.

Upon reaching the time of 4 weeks after conception, the perception changed: I was a consciousness and perception that formed a sphere (of life force) *and protruded beyond my mother's womb about 10cm.*

At 3 weeks after conception, this sphere was much larger (diameter about 1.5 m) *and the sphere seemed to revolve around its center, which was anchored in my mother's womb.*

At 2 weeks after my conception, this sphere was even larger (diameter about 4m) and my consciousness was like a sphere within this sphere on an orbit, creating a kind of vortex.

1 week after my conception this state was about the same, only the anchoring still felt very loose.

At the time of my conception, I was near my parents and could sense their feelings. I briefly wondered if this was indiscreet now, but since I was in a sense the main person in this event, I decided it was o.k. that way.

When I then returned to the time before my procreation, I saw my soul absorbed in itself in a heavy, serious, almost depressed mood and I wondered if all souls feel this way shortly before the procreation of their future body.

I had the feeling that Jörg could now come next to me, since I was now outside my memories as Harry and we were now in the familiar realm of dream travel. I asked Jörg about it and when he agreed, I sent a beam of light from me to him to mark the way to me. When the ray of light arrived at him, I had the feeling that I should give him my hand along the ray of light (only in the vision, not with my material hand)

and pull him over to me.

During this being pulled over, Jörg had the feeling to be pulled through several pages of the Egyptian Book of the Dead.

When he was then next to me, we looked at my soul and Jörg pointed out to me that the soul is sitting here in front of a place which looks like an arena. On our questions to the arena about its nature Jörg received the answer 'preparation' and I 'place of silence' – thus a place of silent preparation of the souls for their next incarnation.

On my question to the 'place of silence' where I could receive information about my decision to lead this life, I was directed by him to a place far behind me. Jörg and I turned around and flew there. I saw a large round sphere whose surface had large streaks, as if from a slow-flowing liquid.

"Apache tear," said Jörg (=smoke obsidian).

"Fits well," I replied, "in stone healing, smoke obsidian is the stone that brings you back to what you originally once wanted. And the streaks in the surface of the sphere really do resemble the flowing lava from which the smoke obsidian is formed. – Look, there's a space inside the sphere and a seat of sorts. I'm going to go inside."

"I'll stay outside – the place is not approved for me."

"Yes, I feel that way too."

On the seat in this sphere I felt again the heaviness in the 'mind' of the soul, which I had felt in it also already at the 'place of silence'.

When I had united with my soul and was sitting there in the sphere on the seat, I could only direct my consciousness forward to the coming incarnation – apparently my soul was exclusively occupied with the decision for this incarnation while sitting on this seat in this sphere.

I did not manage to get more concrete information from it about the reason for this coming (my present) *life. However, upon my question to my soul, a kind of light rays appeared behind me on the left, pointing to the information I wanted.*

"We have to go further, Jörg, here the information does not exist yet."

We flew toward the source of this light and were surprised to see a huge, white-radiant building teeming with equally white-radiant people in and in front of it. The tower-like building was far larger than anything previously seen in man-made buildings.

When we tried to enter the building, we felt that it was forbidden for us to do so.

"Only dead people are allowed to enter," said Jörg, "unless you meet certain conditions."

"What conditions?"

"I don't know."

"Who should we ask? The gatekeeper of the house?"

"Yes, that's what I was thinking."

There was a big crowd outside the gatekeeper's window and it took me a while to get to the window and ask the gatekeeper my question.

"The condition is that every living person who learns the reason for his incarnation must follow his truth."

When I shared this answer with Jörg, he agreed with me: "I received as an answer that after entering this house, the residual freedom one has due to his ignorance disappears and one is bound to his decision (to life one's current incarnation).*"*

After a short consideration I decided to accept this condition and told this to the gatekeeper, whereupon I was allowed to enter the house.

Jörg told me that he had to stay outside, but that he could see inside the house, since we had already been in this building before this time. The house had looked somewhat different then, on our earlier dream journey here to Chesed.

"It's strange how many 'dead' people there are – you don't usually realize that … and they look more alive than the living." Jörg commented.

There were also a lot of white-glowing people in the building. I wished my way to the right place in the building and arrived in a large, high, elongated room, which reminded me of a Gothic church. In this room there was a lot of fear in the middle third (of the height).

When I looked at the front wall of the room, a large picture appeared there, making the room look like a movie theater. On the 'screen' I could see a landscape passing by that looked familiar. Then came a scene in which I could see my death in one of my past lives, of which I had already had some visions.

"Look at the walls," said Jörg, "there are faces there."

As I looked up at the side walls, I also saw these faces and I recognized them as my previous incarnations, some of which I had already seen on previous dream journeys. As I looked at them and thought how much fear there is, one of the faces corrected me: "Fear, greed and hate!"

(Thes three fundamental problems of man according to Buddhism are greed, hatred and delision.)

Somewhat perplexed, I looked around.

"This room is not only a 'cinema,' but also a 'library,'" Jörg commented.

As I pondered where in this room I could find the information about my soul's intention for my present life, I sensed a large, bright, white light at the front above the room, which Jörg could also see shining in the upper third of the building, and whose name I spontaneously recognized as 'Wisdom'.

Speaking to this light was very easy and the answers came very clearly. I wished myself to the place at which the light was. From the outside this light seemed to be almost endless; from the inside (when I connected with the light) *its boundaries were clear. It had no inner structure, only this outer border, which one could hardly see from the outside.*

I said to Jörg: "I believe this light is the highest form, which a living being can take, which is still delimited."

When I asked this light for the desired information, it showed me a place on the wall of the room where the light was.

"Behind it lies the knowledge, the knowledge of your whole life."

"If I want to know the intention for my present life, does that mean I will know the entire course of my present life?"

"Yes."

"Um, I think I will ponder about that for a while – I'd rather not rush into that."

I thanked him and went back out to Jörg: "Knowing the entire course of my life is quite strange after all – it completely changes your perspective."

"Yes, then freedom disappears, just as the gatekeeper said it would."

"It rather shifts from the level of my psyche to the level of my soul."

"The apparent freedom or limited freedom during life then becomes the freedom of the decision to live this life."

"Well, it also fits with this: that by this knowledge one becomes bound to fidelity to one's own truth."

"Is there anything important to do here, Jörg, before we return? – I think there's something up ahead on the left where we should go again."

We came to a sort of pond or fountain surrounded by a good knee-high wall, with another small circular wall in the middle.

Jörg: "What is the name of the place?"

"I get 'Lake of Memories' as an answer."

"What are we supposed to do here?"

"Put our hand in it or drink from it."

"Throw a coin in it."

"So it seems to be about a symbolic contact. And it seems to be important that not only one of us, but both of us make this contact."

So we both bent over the water and made contact. I saw a Chinese-style dragon and Jörg saw war scenes. As we talked about it, the two sceneries began to change.

Jörg: "Since it seems to be important for both of us, let's go in."

"All right."

The scene immediately became clearer and we stood before a dragon that enveloped us in its fire.

"The fire signifies a blessing with strength, Jörg."

I put a hand on the dragon's scales and felt the smoothly scoured, shiny horn scales and the elongated ridges and burrs on it and said in wonder, "Funny, I've never touched a dragon before."

Then I almost had to laugh when I realized what I had said.

After a while we returned upstairs in front of the well. There we felt that it was important in this case to return exactly the same way we had come. Which we then did.

The 'sphere' in which I saw myself in the first four weeks after my conception consist of the 'substance' of the psyche, that is, life force.

The "life force sphere" can be felt quite clearly in pregnant women in the first 3-4 weeks, and from this the pregnancy of the woman can be recognized.

The place of silence in this vision is called "Tiphareth" on the Tree of Life – the area of the individual soul.

The ball of smoke obsidian on the Tree of Life is called "Geburah" – the realm of karma, i.e. the soul's motivation for its current incarnation. The dragon we met on the way back also belongs to this realm.

The great building on the Tree of Life is called "Chesed" – the realm of transparency, where all information can be found. This area is sometimes called "akasha chronicle".

The akasha chronicle, i.e. the hall of memories of previous incarnations, is a detailed variant of the experience that sometimes occurs during the dream journey to one's own center: the persons who have found their own soul (Tiphareth) sometimes go further until they come to a circle of people who appear to this person like brothers and sisters (Chesed) – although only in the rarest cases it becomes immediately clear to the dream travelers that these are their figures in their own previous incarnations.

The faces on the walls of this hall were my previous incarnations.

The 'dead' we saw in Chesed looked more alive than the living because they were only souls without psyches and therefore the radiance of the souls has not been dimmed by the fears, addictions and self-doubts in the psyche.

The well is the beginning of the path between Chesed and Geburah – just like the ray of light we followed from the 'Apache Tear' to the 'big building' to Chesed.

From the soul it is easy to look into the psyche, but from the psyche most people can only look into the realm of the soul from time to time until they are about 5 years old. After that, the border between psyche and soul remains largely opaque until one has harmonized and healed one's own psyche to the greatest possible extent.

This effect leads to the fact that although the soul can see all its previous incarnations, the waling consciousness within a single incarnation can still remember its own soul during the first five years, but after that it forgets it and can no longer see its previous incarnations. This memory is usually regained only by meditations and dream journeys.

The inner voice, which sometimes can speak very clearly to a person and usually gives the central indications in one's life, probably comes here from Chesed from the light of wisdom. This light of wisdom, that is the essence of one's own soul and all its previous incarnations, gives, so to speak, at the essential points in one's life, supporting directing instructions for the normal waking consciousness in the world –

telepathy from the wisdom of the soul to the everyday waking consciousness.

I have not yet looked at the rest of my life, but presumably this will happen at some point – which means that I will then shift my center from my psyche to my soul, so that my soul will then become my identity instead of my psyche. Such a serious transformation, it seems to me, should be approached only after careful consideration and good preparation.

The area into which this dream journey has led is the area in which the Tulkus are at home and in which they have become fully perceptive and fully capable of acting. The Tulkus are the approximately 1000 Tibetan monks who are able to, on the one hand, remember their previous lives (including the knowledge they possessed at that time) and, on the other hand, foresee and predict their future lives.

This information can be obtained in the "big building" in a dream journey to this Chesed building. This place can of course look a little different for every dream traveler, but the inner structure is the same, because it results from the function of this place.

Of course, it is not necessary to make a dream journey to this area if you want to get to know it, but a dream journey is a quite reliable and simple method to make a first contact.

It is also by no means done with the dream journey, because one will only be able to receive and endure and even enjoy the "omniscience" when one no longer fears anything that lies in feelings and images in one's own subconscious. These unhealed images are what make the psyche opaque, that is, make parts of it unconscious – which ultimately hinders telepathy.

The "perfect telepathy" requires first a perfect healing of the own psyche.

Strictly speaking, telepathy in the sense of correspondence between inside and outside is always perfectly there – it is only the awareness of these connections and of the whole world that is normally limited.

Dream journeys in pairs are a way to achieve greater concentration than dream journeys undertaken alone. For larger or more important undertakings that lead into new territory, such as here the journey to one's own soul to ask it about its intention for this incarnation, such "team dream journeys" are therefore recommended.

On these journeys both dream travelers are in the same image and talk to each other during the journey, i.e. they talk normally with their mouths and not telepathically. However, the images that both see are telepathically coordinated – as evidenced by the fact that one often sees something that the other then speaks out before one could say anything about it oneself.

7. c) A step-way meditation

One can use the most different systems to come to such experiences as the dream journey just described. Since one also comes closer to the all-encompassing "telepathy web", such dream journeys and meditations are also an aid to further one's own telepathic abilities – this method is indirect, since one does not specifically practice telepathy, but it is nevertheless effective, since one thereby becomes more familiar with the area in which telepathy takes place.

The simplest approach to such dream journeys and meditations is the idea of walking step by step in one's own imagination along one of the gradual paths that lead from the multiplicity in the here and now to the unity that underlies everything. In doing so, it is, of course, most useful to begin by using a path with which one is already familiar. This can be, as already mentioned, the ladder of heaven of the Christian mystics, the cabbalistic tree of life of the Jewish mystics, the rose path of the Sufis, the yoga system of the Yogis, the Lamrim of the Tibetan Lamas or any other of the many systems that exist for this path.

The North Indian and Tibetan mandala meditations are also a step-by-step path: First, a concentric image is sketched that contains all aspects of the world. Then all the meditator's memories are placed in this mandala, so that he sees himself and the whole world in this mandala. Finally, from the multiplicity of appearances in the outer circle of the mandala, he passes through several circles containing more and more fundamental symbols, until he reaches the unity in the center of the mandala, which is the source and essence of all the multiplicity of the world.

The astrological system of planets is not suitable as a basis for this path, but the sequence of planets from Moon to Pluto is nevertheless quite similar to this path.

This stepwise path exists not only in the various mystical, magical and religious systems, but also in today's physics. Since physics is the basis of today's worldview, a Step Path meditation based on this worldview is best anchored in reality, i.e. the Path as such is experienced as real. Therefore, the use of the physical worldview is particularly well suited for this form of meditation.

The use of physics as "picture" and basis for a mandala, i.e. for a step way meditation has the practical advantage that one has already defined the outer circle of the mandala, i.e. the first step: The whole world is physics or consists of physical things.

In the following, some details have been omitted in the presentation of this physical step path; only the straight path from multiplicity to unity has been presented. If one is well versed in physics, one can add as many more details as one likes to the path.

This meditation has the following stages, which one contemplates each time until one sees and feels inwardly, "Yes, it is so."

The world consists of the universe – the earth is a part of the world and you yourself are a living being on the earth.

One's own body is made up of organs.

The organs are made of cells.

The cells consist of molecules.

The molecules consist of atoms.

The atoms consist of the atomic nucleus and the electrons.

The atomic nuclei consist of protons and of neutrons.

The protons and the neutrons consist of three quarks each.

The elementary particles, i.e. the quarks, electrons and neutrinos, are also energy quanta according to the formula "$E=mc^2$". There are three types of them: gravitons (energy quanta of gravitation), photons (energy quanta of electromagnetic force) and gluons (energy quanta of color force in atomic nuclei).

Energy quanta are curvatures in the space-time. The space-time extends through the whole universe from its beginning to its end – it is, so to speak, the paper on which the picture of the universe has been stamped: Each energy quantum is a small dent in this "space-time paper".

The space is a sequence of states of the time – the time is the real thing. It always takes new forms, which show up as the state of the world in a certain moment. Space is a snapshot of time.

From this there are two important pairs of conclusion:

Space-time is the outside of the unity.
Consciousness, that is the inside of this space-time, is God.

My body is a part of the space-time.
My consciousness is a part of God.

It is helpful to do this contemplation often and to remain aware that you are also contemplating yourself in the world.

This step-by-step path corresponds to the steps of the Kabbalistic Tree of Life, on which one can therefore also map this physical path. The correspondence between the physical step way and the tree of life is very precise: Both are an eleven-part model, which has the same properties – the tree of life has eleven "spheres" and the physical superstring theory has eleven mathematical dimensions.

The beginning is God or the time dimension.

The second realm is the three God spheres or the three extended space dimensions.

The third realm is the three soul spheres or the first triad of non-extended, i.e., "hidden" space dimensions.

The fourth area are the three psyche spheres or the second group of three non-extended, i.e. "hidden" space dimensions.

The end is the body-sphere or the eleventh dimension, which summarizes the other ten dimensions.

This correspondence, which is described here only very briefly, shows that there are the same structures on the "inside of the world", in which telepathy is located, as on the "outside of the world", which is described by physics – both are after all the same world …

A more detailed consideration on this subject with many examples of such coinciding structures in physics and in the spiritual-magical-astrological realm can be found in my book "The Synthesis of Physics and Magic".

7. d) Consciousness and matter

This correspondence between the physical step path and the spiritual step path of the Tree of Life shows that consciousness is the inside of the world and matter is the outside of the world.

If this description is taken literally, there are four types of action in the world:

Matter acts on matter: I take an apple and eat it.

Matter acts on consciousness: I see a friend and rejoice.

Consciousness acts on matter: I turn a paper wheel with the help of tele-kinesis (see the experiment in "Telekinesis for Beginners").

Consciousness acts on consciousness: I sense that someone is staring at me from behind.

This simple model of the two sides of the world (inside = consciousness; outside = matter) can make it easier to place telepathic and telekinetic experiences into a more comprehensive world view and not to experience telepathy and telekinesis as contradictory to the physical world view.

8. The Use of the "Telepathy Level"

8. a) The use of telepathy on a large scale

The acquaintance with telepathy begins with the first experiences and experiments, which show that telepathy really exists.

Next come the experiments, with the help of which the essence of telepathy is investigated in more detail, and the first attempts to use telepathy concretely in every-day life. Very likely this will then develop into a more or less systemic form of magic.

Finally the question arises, how one can use telepathy generally in one's own life organization. Here there are a number of different approaches.

The best known is probably the principle of "the hundredth monkey": If a certain number of people or animals have learned something, this ability expands to all people or animals at once – without them having seen or heard of this ability anywhere physically.

If enough people or animals know something, this knowledge begins to radiate, so to speak, in the collective subconsciousness in such a way that all people can perceive this knowledge telepathically and apply it.

This principle is often used to meditate collectively for world peace or the like. The basic idea is that if enough people concentrate on one motive, this motive becomes conscious to all others via the collective subconsciousness and is enacted after this by all people. One could regard this as a kind of self-hypnosis or self-programming of mankind.

Unfortunately, demagogues and dictators also use this principle. The best known is probably Hitler's "Cooptation of the German People".

You can also base your own life on this principle. Thus I've lived for more than fifteen years from consultations and from writing books. I do not adver-tise and do not charge anyone for my consultations, but simply accept the donations I receive for them. In this way, what I do reaches those who need it, not those who have a lot of money.

If I am ever in need of money, I tell "those up there," that is, my soul, the gods etc., who have always helped me so far – and they always have helped me. So you can also base your own livelihood on telepathy – you could also say that you can trust life, the gods and (if you want to call it like that) telepathy in this point, too: What you need will come if you trust in life.

This principle of trust sends out images of the "good state" telepathically – and these images then call forth the "good things". Of course, this works only if one really trusts, and not if one only "wants to trust" – and makes an effort for the maintenance of this trust every day.

On the level of telepathy there is no lie, but only the image that one carries within oneself and sends out. The image of a fear, which one has wrapped with trust and passes off as trust, will evoke fear, because this image is fear at its core after all.

For telepathy, a basic sincerity is necessary, otherwise one summons things that are not what one wanted to meet. Telepathy always sees what is in the whole package of a topic and summons that.

One could build an entire economic system on telepathy if enough people in that system developed a sufficiently great sense of trust and responsibility.

Then it would be possible to wish for what you need and trust that it will come. Some things could be shared. And one would act in such a way that it is good for all.

In all economic systems today, money is what regulates supply and demand, that is, coordinates the making of goods with people's need for goods. Unfortunately, this creates primarily a struggle for money rather than general cooperation to ensure that the most useful and enduring products are produced and that these products get to those who need them.

This role of coordinator, which money has today, could be taken over by the collective subconsciousness, i.e. by telepathy, in an economic form which is sufficiently supported by trust and responsibility. In this kind of economy telepathy would bring in contact those, which have something spare or would like to produce, with those, which need the concerning – one would meet simply by "telepathically caused meaningful coincidences".

One can begin this kind of economy simply in the small scale and wish oneself those things, which one needs – and give those things to others or do that for them, which these need (if one possesses this and/or gladly does this).

More about this kind of economy may be found in my books "Money Magic for Beginners" und "Von innerer Fülle zu äußerem Gedeihen".

8. b) Shaping your own life

Even in the general application of telepathy there is no patent remedy that is valid for everyone. In the end, everyone has to ask himself how he wants to use telepathy in his life. This depends to a large extent also on how sure one has become of the existence of telepathy and how much confidence one has therefore developed.

Presumably, it will also become easier to incorporate telepathy into one's life as a permanent grounding when there are more people than at present for whom telepathy has become something completely real and normal – and who also talk about their experiences with others. Then telepathy will become common everyday knowlegde.

Since these people will most likely use telepathy in very different ways, it will then also become easier to find a role model whose approach is also suitable for oneself.

A little further on in the development, the basic principles of the new world view, in which telepathy has been fully integrated, will also crystallize. Probably trust and responsibility will be two essential elements in this world view, since these two qualities are the two sides of one's telepathic connection with the world: In trust one is borne by the world and in responsibility one bears the world.

So far such a telepathically carried way of life including a telepathically coordinated economic system is designed and described in more detail mainly in science fiction novels: The Planet of the Wise, who live peacefully and communicate and coordinate their actions telepathically. This is quite a real possibility – but until this will be a reality on earth, it will probably still take a while …

As Confucius so aptly said, "Even the longest journey begins with the first step." If you take a first step in the right direction, after that the second step becomes clear, then the third … and so you keep moving forward.

Consequently, you don't have to know the whole path to get to your destination, but you do have to get started.

This is also true for learning telepathy.

And it is helpful to approach it playfully rather than seriously and sacrificially.

9. The History of Telepathy

9. a) From the Stone Age until today

Life can be divided into seven phases – both the history of mankind and the individual biography.

1.

In the beginning there is the oral phase – the infant puts everything into its mouth and lives completely in the security of its mother.

This corresponds in history to the Paleolithic Age, when people lived in nature as part of nature.

This period can be characterized by a "Yes".

In this epoch of complete connectedness with everything, telepathy is the most normal thing of all – after all, everything is connected with everything (association) and the individual is secure in the whole and especially with his mother and with the 'Great Mother'.

2.

This is followed by the anal phase – the infant learns to talk and walk and to want things and to reject other things.

A distinction between 'wanted' and 'rejected' also emerges in the Neolithic period: on one side, the village, gardens, farmland and pastures, and on the other side, the wilderness.

This period can be characterized by a "No!".

In this epoch of discernment, of cycles (especially of agriculture) and of the right order of all things, telepathy becomes a part of the all-pervading and all-supporting "rightness" described by the rules of behavior and by the myths. Following this order makes survival possible. Telepathy evolves in this epoch from the attachment to the mother and to the mother goddess to the attachment to rightness and to a multitude of gods.

3.

Next comes the phallic stage – the child recognizes itself as an independent being and learns to say "I".

At the end of the Neolithic period, kingship has emerged and with it monotheism and philosophy – everything is directed towards or derived from the king, a center, an origin, the one God.

This time can be characterized by an "I!!!". From the "Yes" the "No!" has arisen and both together make the recognition of the "I!!!" possible.

In this epoch everything starts from the king and from God. In the Old Stone Age telepathy was the connection with the mother and the mother goddess; in the New Stone Age telepathy was the being borne by the all-embracing right order; in kingship and the monotheism telepathy is connected with being inserted into the total system which is centrally steered by God or by the king as his representative.

4.

The phallic phase passes into the genital phase – the adolescent explores the world and the opposite sex.

Kingship is replaced by materialism, which also explores the world and uses it. The gaze now becomes completely outward to the world, relegating the inside to the background.

This period can be characterized by a "You?" that follows the "Me!!!" of the previous phase.

In this epoch also telepathy fades completely into the background, because only analyzing and producing is done and not looking for the inner connections. This is the first age, in which the telepathy was ignored to a large extent and in which it became therefore necessary to prove first of all its existence.

5.

Now follows the adult phase – the adult has chosen a partner for the foundation of a family and establishes in mutual trust and responsibility a community in which one is connected with each other.

This corresponds to the presently beginning epoch of globalization, in which all must share the consequences of the deeds of all others. It is time to create on earth a "family of peoples" in which all can continue to live in their own way and at the same time have the well-being of the whole in mind.

This time can be characterized by a "We." that results from the "I!!!" and the "You?".

In this epoch telepathy is something that is urgently needed and therefore it is rediscovered, developed and integrated – after all telepathy coordinates the individuals to a community. The family and also the "family of peoples" is a system in which all depend on all others. Such a system can only flourish in trust and responsibility – and the inside of these connections between all is telepathy.

The two phases that still follow in biography, are historically still in the future:

6.

These first of these two future phases is the tutorial phase of teaching in advanced age. This is also an epochs of magic and religion: telepathy becomes a connection with the gods and with the disciples.

The tutorial phase can be characterized by "Other …".

7.

These second of these two future phases is the gerontal phase of wisdom of old age. This is also an epochs of magic and religion: telepathy becomes a connection with God.

The gerontal phase can be characterized by "All." From the union of the "We" and the "Other …" emerges the "All."

This development can be described by just seven words: "Yes" – "No!" – "I!!!" – "You?" – "We." – "Other …" – "All."

The conception of telepathy in these seven stages is quite different:

"Yes."	security in the Great Mother
"No!"	being borne by the all-embracing right order
"I!!!"	being included in the hierarchy directed by God.
"You?"	extensive ignoring of telepathy
"We."	coordination of individuals into one family
"Other …"	becoming familiar with the strange and the stranger
"All."	experiencing all-connectedness and unity.

9. b)   One's own development

One's own development of telepathy depends on one's age and on the culture in which one lives. The clearly stronger formative element is the culture and its relation to telepathy: In a community where telepathy is something quite normal, one will use telepathy at any age – simply because it is such a practical tool.

In addition, of course, there is the importance that telepathy has acquired in one's own life – not everyone is a seer and uses telepathy professionally. But everyone can experience telepathy as an element on which one's trust in life is based: Things do not happen randomly, but in relation to each other, which means, among other things, that the inner healing also entails a healing of the outer life situation.

Telepathy coordinates the inner images with the outer events.

10.   Forms of Telepathy

10. a)   Possibilities

In the two volumes "Telepathy for Beginners" and "Telepathy for Advanced" a number of different telepathic experiences have been described. It is therefore useful to take a closer look at these different experiences and see if they can be put together to form a vivid picture of telepathic possibilities.

unintentional telepathy

unintentional spatial perception in dreams

One can see in a dream what has been imagined in another room. Probably this case is more frequent – especially the dream-perception of the actions of another person who is doing something that is significant for the dreamer.

unintentional, semiconscious spatial perception

The best known example of this form of telepathy is the ability to sense when someone else is staring at you from behind.

Presumably, unconscious telepathy is relatively common – but since it is unconscious, it usually goes unnoticed …

unintentional, conscious spatial perception

In the case of conscious, but unintentional telepathic perception one sees e.g. all at once what another person has experienced e.g. on vacation and what he is talking about. You can also hear what another person is thinking or what he is wishing for, or you can see how another person is feeling.

A little more special is the telepathic recognition of what has been imagined in a room during a meditation or a ritual.

Another special form of this kind of telepathy is the perception and interpretation of an omen, that is, the recognition that a strange event has a meaning.

unintentional temporal perception in dreams

A prophetic dream, i.e. a dream in which one foresees something (which usually happens the next day) is unintentional and semi-conscious (dream).

unintentional, unconscious sending

Unintentional telepathic sending by a human being is known especially in connection with PCs, which sometimes react quite violently to the stress of their users.

Again, most cases of telepathic sending are likely to be unknown, precisely because they are unconscious.

Life force vampirism is not sending but sucking, but since both are "moving of life force", it can be added to the unintentional sending – although there is of course also the intentional life force sucking.

intentional telepathy

intentional, but unconscious perception

In this form of telepathy, a "monitor" is used, that is, an aid by which the subconscious mind, having obtained the information telepathically, transmits this information to the waking conscious mind.

This tool can be a pendulum, the own fingers, the "zombie-experiment", automatic writing, automatic speaking or also quite classically an oracle.

conscious, intentional spatial perception

One can intentionally and consciously with the help of telepathy find lost objects, find a way, recognize the whereabouts of someone else, correctly diagnose an engine failure, draw the jackpot ticket, etc.

A dream journey is such a telepathic seeing, which has a somewhat more defined external form.

An already more advanced form of telepathy is the conscious and intentional shifting with one's own consciousness into the body of another person in order to examine the condition of the organs or chakras of the other and possibly also to heal them.

Intentional foreseeing of the future is known by almost all cultures: the seers and seeresses.

A special form are the tulkus, who can remember their past lives as well as foresee their next life.

conscious, intentional sending

One can purposefully send an image or word to another – even immediately after birth. Animals also respond to telepathic sending of images.

Telepathically summoning another person transitions into remote hypnosis, which is a form of hypnotizing another person who is not present.

Summoning things, events and experiences is a formless variant of magic, which is, so to speak, "effective wishing in ritual form".

Telekinesis can be added to intentional sending, even though it involves not just sending a thought or an image, but triggering a physical effect.

Whether a poltergeist causes its effect intentionally, is difficult to fathom – to fathom that, one would have to be at least able to talk to the poltergeist about that …

One could also count homeopathy among the forms of intentional telepathic sending, even if the actual effect does not come from the sender, i.e. from the homeopath, but from the homeopathic remedy.

The forms of telepathy listed here also include intentional vital force vampirism, i.e. intentional sucking of the vital force of another person.

perfect telepathy

perfect perception from the outside

In astral travel, one leaves one's own body with one's consciousness and with one's perceptive faculty and flies to any other place and perceives it as clearly as with the physical senses.

The transmission of consciousness called "Phowa" in Tibet is an extreme case of this kind of telepathy. In this process, a yogi who is about to die leaves his physical body with his astral body and seeks out the body of a recently deceased young person, revives this body and then takes it over as his own body for some time.

perfect perception from within

During the dream journey to the "house of omniscience" ("akasha chronicle"), in which one can see, among other things, one's former incarnations, one is in an "inward place", i.e. not in an outward place as in the astral journey.

group telepathy

unintentional collective coordination

This form of telepathy has become known mainly by the phenomenon of the "100th monkey" – this is a special form of swarm intelligence, which can be observed, for example, in the synchronized movements of fish in a school of fish.

Two negative variants of this possibility of collective telepathic coordination are mass psychosis and mass panic.

A small group variant is telepathic coordination while thinking or exploring a topic.

intentional collective coordination

Collective telepathic coordination is used primarily in group dream journeys and in family constellations, as well as in joint meditations of larger groups of people.

The "postcard experiment" is a simple experiment to prove telepathy, where several people work together.

The negative variant of intentional collective telepathy is political or religious propaganda.

impersonal collective coordination

Astrology, by its non-physical effects, is also a form of telepathy. It works both individually through the horoscope and collectively through the current planetary position.

One can represent the forms of telepathy described here with a simple scheme:

Forms of telepathy				
Awareness	**Intention**			
	unintentional	*intentional*	*perfect*	*impersonal*
unconscious	sending	spatial perception		
in dreams	spatial perception			
	temporal perception			
semiconsciously	spatial perception			
collective	coordination	coordination		coordination (astrology)
conscious	spatial perception	spatial perception		
	temporal perception	temporal perception		
		sending (and sucking)		
			spatial perception from outside	
			spatial-temporal perception from the inside	

Telepathy begins with the unconscious forms, which partly take place in dreams.

In the semi-conscious forms of telepathy, one is capable of a reaction, but one is not fully aware of it (being stared at from behind).

The collective forms of telepathy are conscious from the sender's side, but mostly unconscious from the receiver's side – which is quite intentional, especially in propaganda.

Conscious telepathy is the most comprehensive: In it there is both spatial and temporal telepathic perception as well as the two perfect forms of telepathy.

What might a perfect collective coordination look like? With the help of meditations and dream journeys, on the step-path a little above the "Hall of Omniscience" one can find an area where a community meets, where all are connected with all and are safe in this community. Possibly this is a place of perfect collective coordination.

On the Tree of Life, this place is called "Binah."

A distinct difference in the experience of telepathy exists between astral projection and dream journeys (including the omniscience state in the "akasha chronicle").

> In astral projection one sees things "optically" a little differently than with the physical eyes, but one sees the outer, physical world. One also has this kind of "seeing" when one telepathically searches for a lost object, changes with one's consciousness into another person and looks at his organs, or when one suddenly sees before oneself the scenes of the vacation memories about which another person is just reporting.
>
> Astral projection is the perfect, clear form of this kind of telepathic perception, in which one looks at things from the outside. In normal telepathy the vision is usually a little bid "shadowy" and "clouded".

> The perception in dream journeys is clearly different: it can be both symbolic-dreamlike and concrete-real. The kind of images depends on the orientation: For example, if one travels to one's own center or to a deity, the images will be symbolic – on the other hand, if one travels to Egypt, for example, one will find the pyramids there as well. However, the tendency to symbolic images is very pronounced in dream journeys, since one may see, for example, the pyramids not as they look today, but as they have been at the time of their builders.
>
> While in telepathic search and in astral journey one immediately sees things "from the outside", in dream travel one perceives things "from the inside", unless one makes an effort to perceive them "from the outside".

In telepathic search and in astral projection one travels, so to speak, with one's perception (telepathic search) or with one's whole astral body (astral projection) in the outer world to the desired place and looks around there, while in the dream journey one travels with one's consciousness, so to speak, on the level of consciousness, i.e. in the "inner world" to the subject about which one wants to learn something.

By telepathic search and astral travel one can learn something about the outer form – by dream journeys one can learn something about the inner meaning of things. For example, if one wants to know whether an organ is sick, one will make a telepathic search, i.e. in this case one will look telepathically at the organ from the outside – but if one wants to know why the organ has become sick, one will make a dream journey to the organ, i.e. one will address it like a living being, whereby one could also use automatic speech.

How to describe precisely and vividly the practical difference between telepathic searching and dream journey? Actually, one can really understand it only by one's own experience. The difference is one's own orientation: Am I going towards something or am I going into something? Am I encountering something or am I becoming something? Do I look at it from the outside or do I look at it from the inside? Am I addressing its substance or am I addressing its consciousness?

In telepathic searching (including astral projection), one goes to something, one encounters something, one looks at it from the outside, and one explores its substance. In dream journeys, you usually go into something, you become something, you look at it from the inside, and you explore its consciousness.

10. b) Applications

In telepathy, the type of consciousness cannot necessarily be willfully determined – but one can practice conscious telepathy and become more sovereign in it.

The distinction between astral projection and telepathic searching on the one hand and dream travel on the other hand will become clearer by itself with increasing experience with telepathy: The appropriate type of telepathic perception and experience will arise of itself from the type of information one is seeking.

11.   Perception and Action

11. a)   Balance

The more one has developed telepathy, that is, the inner ability to perceive, the more important it becomes that one also develops the inner ability to act, that is, telekinesis and magic. If one can see everything but cannot act, the many images flood the psyche to such an extent that one's own autonomy is threatened.

The same is true in reverse: If one becomes more and more effective in wishing and magic, but does not exercise one's perceptive faculty to about the same degree, one may bring about things that one did not want, that one cannot enjoy, or that may even harm one.

A sharp eye and a weak arm are a bad combination – and so are a dull eye and a strong arm …

11. b)   Sorcerer's Apprentice

When one begins to practice telepathy to a greater extent, one should also learn to imprint things by will and imagination. One should aspire to become a seer and a magician at the same time.

Most of the time, one tends to develop one or the other of these two elements much more. To a small extent this does no harm – but if one of the two elements is more than twice as well developed as the other, one should see to it that one brings this imbalance back into balance to some extent.

This hint is already given in "Telepathy for Beginners", but it appears here again, because it is of great importance for one's own well-being.

12.   The First step

12. a)   The step path

Telepathy is the smallest element that can show that the world also contains non-causal connections or non-physical effects. If one examines this element systematically, one finally arrives at a view of the world in which everything is connected with everything else and in which everything resonates with each other in a common rhythm, which results, among other things, from the radiance of the heart and which is described by astrology.

This view of the world is an essential part of the new world view that has begun to develop in the last few decades and will ultimately lead to a "family of nations".

12. b)   One's own way

From an individual point of view, the intensive occupation with telepathy ultimately leads to mysticism, i.e. to a world view in which one experiences oneself as an integrated part of the whole. In this world one is borne by the whole and one bears the whole – which is the essence of the family and the "family of nations".

13. The Original Desire

13. a) Happyness

Is the desire to learn telepathy the primary desire? Or does one want to learn telepathy in order to achieve something with it?

Telepathy in itself has no great value at first – the realization that it exists, of course, changes one's worldview. However, telepathy is not the thing that makes you happy, but it is a tool that can help you to live a happy life – and to experience things that you might have thought impossible before.

13. b) The actual desire

It is therefore useful to ask oneself why one reads the book "Telepathy for Advanced" and possibly also "Telepathy for Beginners".

If the motive has been simple curiosity or thirst for knowledge, it makes sense to perform a resolution ritual for discovering and learning telepathy – as is described in the first chapter of this book.

However, if the motive has been something else for which one wanted to use telepathy as a tool, it makes more sense to directly wish this other thing into one's life. Then one will learn telepathy and wishing along the way and become familiar with this tool.

The direct way is always the most effective and useful way. Choosing this path also allows the soul in one's heart to radiate outward directly and powerfully – and that is ultimately all the soul wants … and it is also what makes the psyche happy.

English Books by Harry Eilenstein

- Living Magic (261 p.)	- Meditation for Beginners
- The Synthesis of Physics and Magic (192 p.)	- Kundalini for Beginners
- Telepathy for Beginners (60 p.)	- Chakra-Magic for Beginners
- Telepathy for Advanced Learners (52 p.)	- Astrology for Beginners
- Telekinesis for Beginners (56 p.)	- Ritual Magic for Beginners
- Astral Projection for Beginners (60 p.)	- Mandalas for Beginners
- Invocations for Beginners (52 p.)	- Love Magic for Beginners
- Evocations for Beginners (62 p.)	- Magic Research for Beginners
- Auto-Movement for Beginners (60 p.)	- Self-awareness for Beginners
- Elves for Beginners (56 p.)	- Symbolism of Numbers for Beginners
- Hypnosis for Beginners (56 p.)	- Language of the Moon – for Beginners
- Money Magic for Beginners (60 p.)	- Magic Chant for Beginners
- Magic Objects for Beginners (64 p.)	- Prophecy for Beginners
- Shamanism for Beginners (52 p.)	- Da'ath-Magic for Beginners
- Number Symbolism for Beginners (64 p.)	- Feng Shui for Beginners
- Crop Circles for Beginners (344 p.)	- Magic for Beginners – Anthology I
	- Magic for Beginners – Anthology II
These books will be puplished soon:	- Magic for Beginners – Anthology III
	- Magic for Beginners – Anthology IV
- Life Force for Beginners	

Bücher von Harry Eilenstein

Religion allgemein
- Die sieben Schritte des Lebens (428 S.)
- Muttergöttin und Schamanen (168 S.)
- Göbekli Tepe (472 S.)
- Die Göttin von Göbekli Tepe (144 S.)
- Totempfähle (440 S.)
- Christus (60 S.)
- Dakini (80 S.)
- Vajra (76 S.)

Ägypten
- Hathor und Re 1: Götter und Mythen im Alten Ägypten (432 S.)
- Hathor und Re 2: Die altägyptische Religion – Ursprünge, Kult und Magie (396 S.)
- Isis (508 S.)

Indogermanen
- Die Entwicklung der indogermanischen Religionen (700 S.)
- Wurzeln und Zweige der indogermanischen Religion (224 S.)

Germanen
- Die Götter der Germanen (87 Bände – siehe nächste Seite)
- Odin (300 S.)

Kelten
- Cernunnos (690 S.)
- Taliesin (228 S.)
- Der Kessel von Gundestrup (220 S.)
- Der Chiemsee-Kessel (76)

Psychologie
- Über die Freude (100 S.)
- Das Geheimnis des inneren Friedens (252 S.)
- Das Beziehungsmandala (52 S.)
- Gefühle und ihre Verwandlungen (404 S.)
- einsgerichtet (140 S.)
- Liebe und Eigenständigkeit (216 S.)
- Von innerer Fülle zu äußerem Gedeihen (52 S.)

Heilung
- Die Symbolik der Krankheiten (76 S.)

Kunst
- Herz des Tanzes – Tanz des Herzens (160 S.)

Drama
- König Athelstan (104 S.)

Bücher von Harry Eilenstein

„Magie für Anfänger"	**Magie**

„Magie für Anfänger"

- Telepathie für Anfänger (60 S.)
- Telepathie für Fortgeschrittene (52 S.)
- Telekinese für Anfänger (52 S.)
- Lebenskraft für Anfänger (60 S.)
- Meditation für Anfänger (56 S.)
- Kundalini für Anfänger (100 S.)
- Hypnose für Anfänger (56 S.)
- Auto-Movement für Anfänger (56 S.)
- Chakra-Magie für Anfänger (148 S.)
- Astralreisen für Anfänger (56 S.)
- Astrologie für Anfänger (120 S.)
- Ritual-Magie für Anfänger (56 S.)
- Mandalas für Anfänger (68 S.)
- Geldzauber für Anfänger (56 S.)
- Liebeszauber für Anfänger (52 S.)
- Invokationen für Anfänger (52 S.)
- Evokationen für Anfänger (60 S.)
- Elfen für Anfänger (56 S.)
- Magie-Forschung für Anfänger (140 S.)
- Selbsterkenntnis für Anfänger (52 S.)
- Zahlensymbolik für Anfänger (60 S.)
- Die Sprache des Mondes – für Anfänger (116 S.)
- Zaubergesänge für Anfänger (100 S.)
- Zukunftschau für Anfänger (60 S.)
- Schamanismus für Anfänger (52 S.)
- Magische Gegenstände für Anfänger (68 S.)
- Da'ath-Magie für Anfänger (64 S.)
- Kornkreise für Anfänger (348 S.)
- Feng Shui für Anfänger (96 S.)
- Magie für Anfänger – Sammelband I (696 S.)
- Magie für Anfänger – Sammelband II (664 S.)
- Magie für Anfänger – Sammelband III (580 S.)

„Traumreisen"

- Traumreisen zu Heilpflanzen (700 S.)

Magie

- Handbuch für Zauberlehrlinge (408 S.)
- Tarot (104 S.)
- Physik und Magie (184 S.)
- Die Synthese von Physik und Magie (200S.)
- Die Magie-Formel (156 S.)
- Krafttiere – Tiergöttinnen – Tiertänze (112 S.)
- Schwitzhütten (524 S.)
- Mythen und Magie der Harfe (116 S.)
- Magie heute – Berichte aus der Praxis (288 S.)

Meditation

- Der Lebenskraftkörper (230 S.)
- Die Chakren (100 S.)
- Das Chakren-System mit den Nebenchakren (296 S.)
- Organe und Chakren (64 S.)
- Die platonischen Körper in den Chakren (156 S.)
- Meditation (140 S.)
- Drachenfeuer (124 S.)
- Kundalini I (676 S.)
- Reinkarnation (156 S.)
- einsgerichtet (140 S.)

Astrologie

- Astrologie (496 S.)
- Photo-Astrologie (428 S.)
- Die astrologischen Aspekte (88 S.)
- Horoskop und Seele (120 S.)

Kabbala

- Kursus der praktischen Kabbala (150 S.)
- Eltern der Erde (450 S.)
- Blüten des Lebensbaumes:
  - Die Struktur des kabbalistischen Lebensbaumes (370 S.)
  - Der kabbalistische Lebensbaum als Forschungshilfsmittel (580 S.)
  - Der kabbalistische Lebensbaum als spirituelle Landkarte (520 S.)

Die Themen der 87 Bände der Reihe „Die Götter der Germanen"

1. Die Entwicklung der germanischen Religion
2. Lexikon der germanischen Religion
3. Der ursprüngliche Göttervater Tyr
4. Tyr in der Unterwelt: der Schmied Wieland
5. Tyr in der Unterwelt: der Riesenkönig   Teil 1
6. Tyr in der Unterwelt: der Riesenkönig   Teil 2
7. Tyr in der Unterwelt: der Zwergenkönig
8. Der Himmelswächter Heimdall
9. Der Sommergott Baldur
10. Der Meeresgott: Ägir, Hler und Njörd
11. Der Eibengott Ullr
12. Die Zwillingsgötter Alcis
13. Der neue Göttervater Odin   Teil 1
14. Der neue Göttervater Odin   Teil 2
15. Der Fruchtbarkeitsgott Freyr
16. Der Chaos-Gott Loki
17. Der Donnergott Thor
18. Der Priestergott Hönir
19. Die Göttersöhne
20. Die unbekannteren Götter
21. Die Göttermutter Frigg
22. Die Liebesgöttin: Freya und Menglöd
23. Die Erdgöttinnen
24. Die Korngöttin Sif
25. Die Apfel-Göttin Idun
26. Die Hügelgrab-Jenseitsgöttin Hel
27. Die Meeres-Jenseitsgöttin Ran
28. Die unbekannteren Jenseitsgöttinnen
29. Die unbekannteren Göttinnen
30. Die Nornen
31. Die Walküren
32. Die Zwerge
33. Der Urriese Ymir
34. Die Riesen
35. Die Riesinnen
36. Mythologische Wesen
37. Mythologische Priester und Priesterinnen
38. Sigurd/Siegfried
39. Helden und Göttersöhne
40. Die Symbolik der Vögel und Insekten
41. Die Symbolik der Schlangen, Drachen und Ungeheuer
42.a Die Symbolik der Herdentiere I
42.b Die Symbolik der Herdentiere II
43. Die Symbolik der Raubtiere
44. Die Symbolik der Wassertiere und sonstigen Tiere
45. Die Symbolik der Pflanzen
46. Die Symbolik der Farben
47. Die Symbolik der Zahlen
48. Die Symbolik von Sonne, Mond und Sternen
49.a Das Jenseits I – Das Hügelgrab
49.b Das Jenseits II – Der Jenseitsweg
50. Seelenvogel, Utiseta und Einweihung
51. Wiederzeugung und Wiedergeburt
52. Elemente der Kosmologie
53. Der Weltenbaum
54. Die Symbolik der Himmelsrichtungen und der Jahreszeiten
55.a Mythologische Motive I
55.b Mythologische Motive II
56. Der Tempel
57. Die Einrichtung des Tempels
58. Priesterin – Seherin – Zauberin – Hexe
59. Priester – Seher – Zauberer
60. Rituelle Kleidung und Schmuck
61. Skalden und Skaldinnen
62 Kriegerinnen und Ekstase-Krieger
63. Die Symbolik der Körperteile
64.a Magie und Ritual I
64.b Magie und Ritual II
64.c Magie und Ritual III
65. Gestaltwandlungen
66.a Magische Angriffs-Waffen
66.b Magische Verteidigungs-Waffen
67. Magische Werkzeuge und Gegenstände
68. Zaubersprüche
69. Göttermet
70. Zaubertränke
71. Träume, Omen und Orakel
72. Runen
73. Sozial-religiöse Rituale
74. Weisheiten und Sprichworte
75. Kenningar
76. Rätsel
77. Die vollständige Edda des Snorri Sturluson
78. Frühe Skaldenlieder
79.a Mythologische Sagas I
79.b Mythologische Sagas II
80. Hymnen an die germanischen Götter